THE WHIMSICAL WATERCOLOR ART OF LAUREL NELSON

A COLORING BOOK

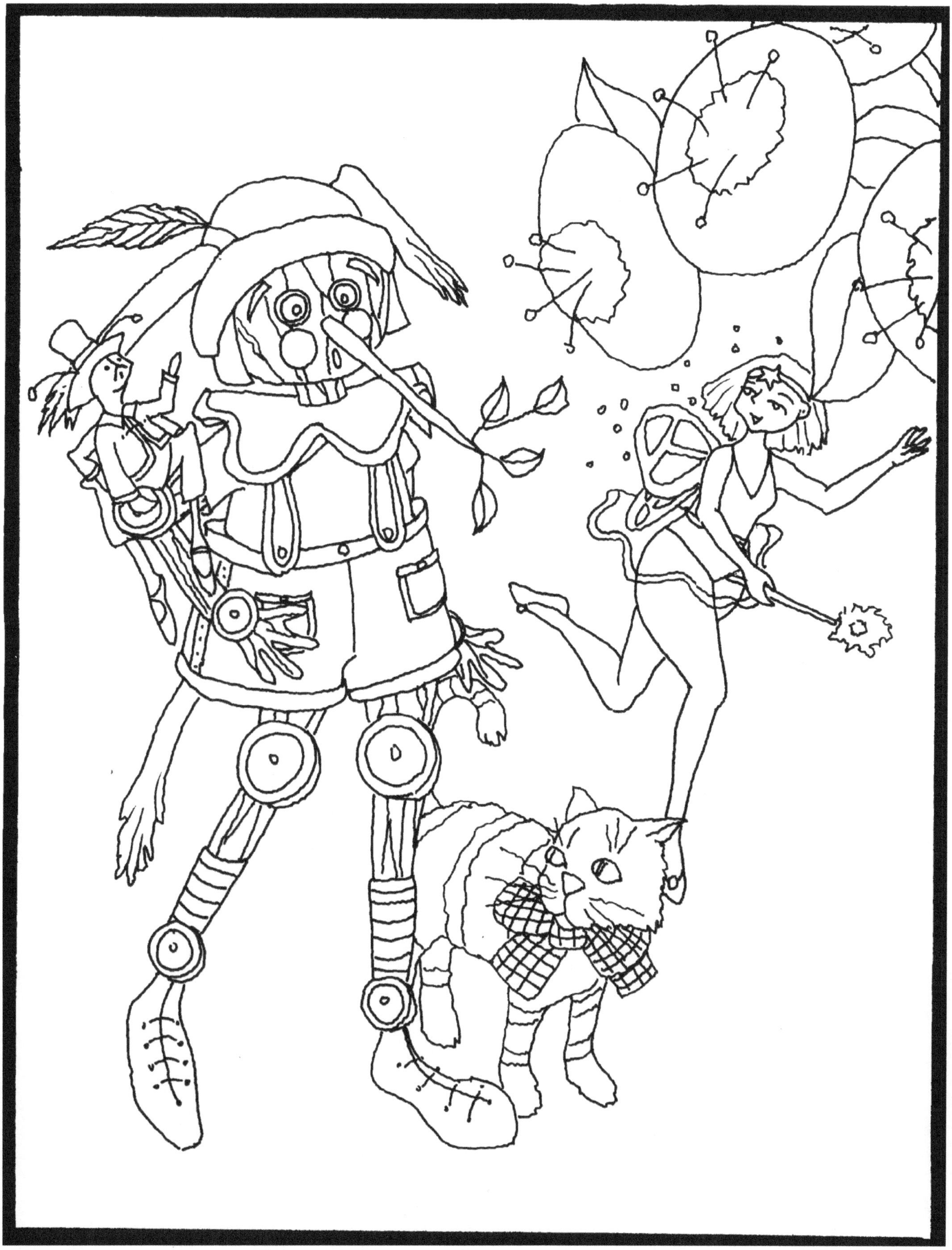

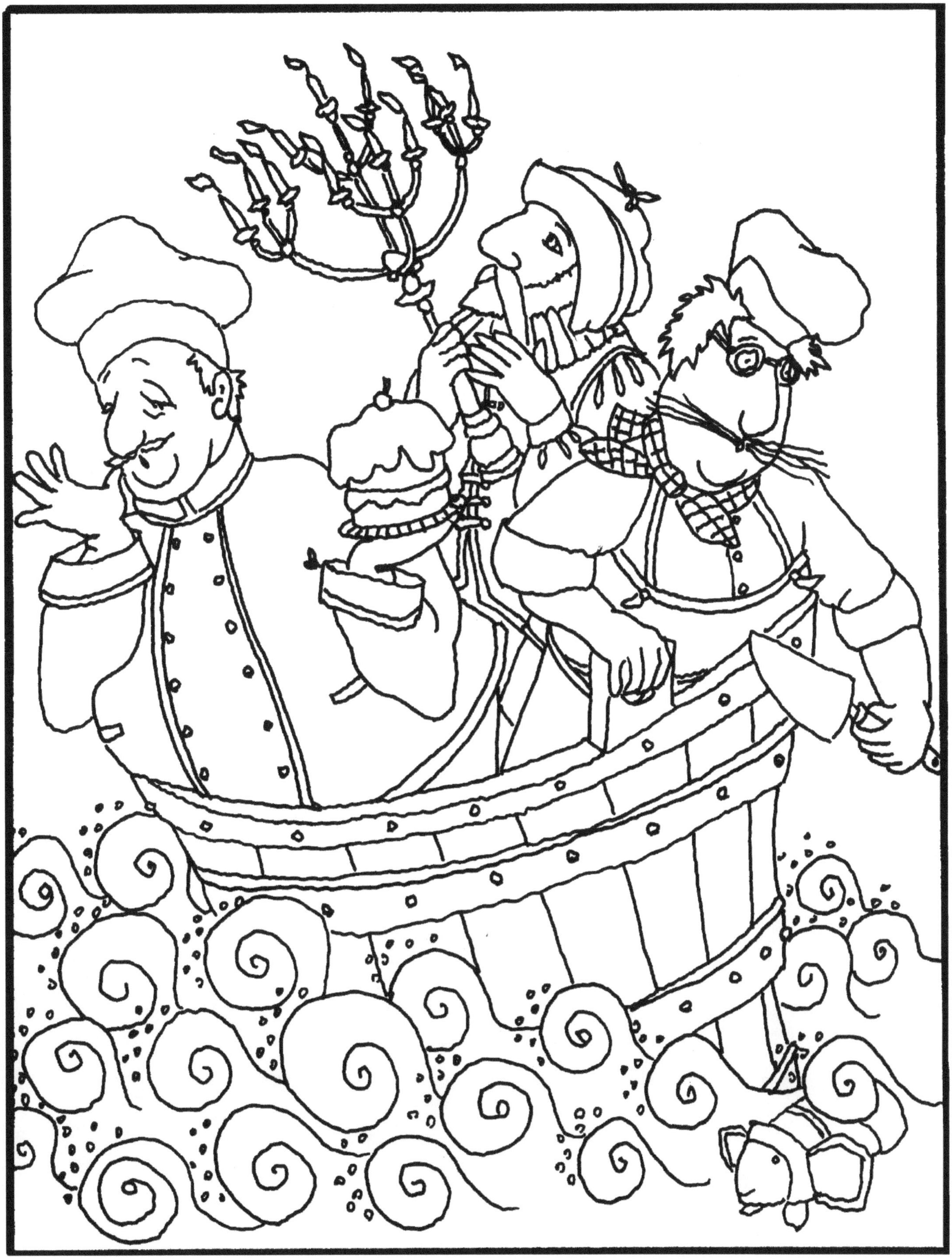

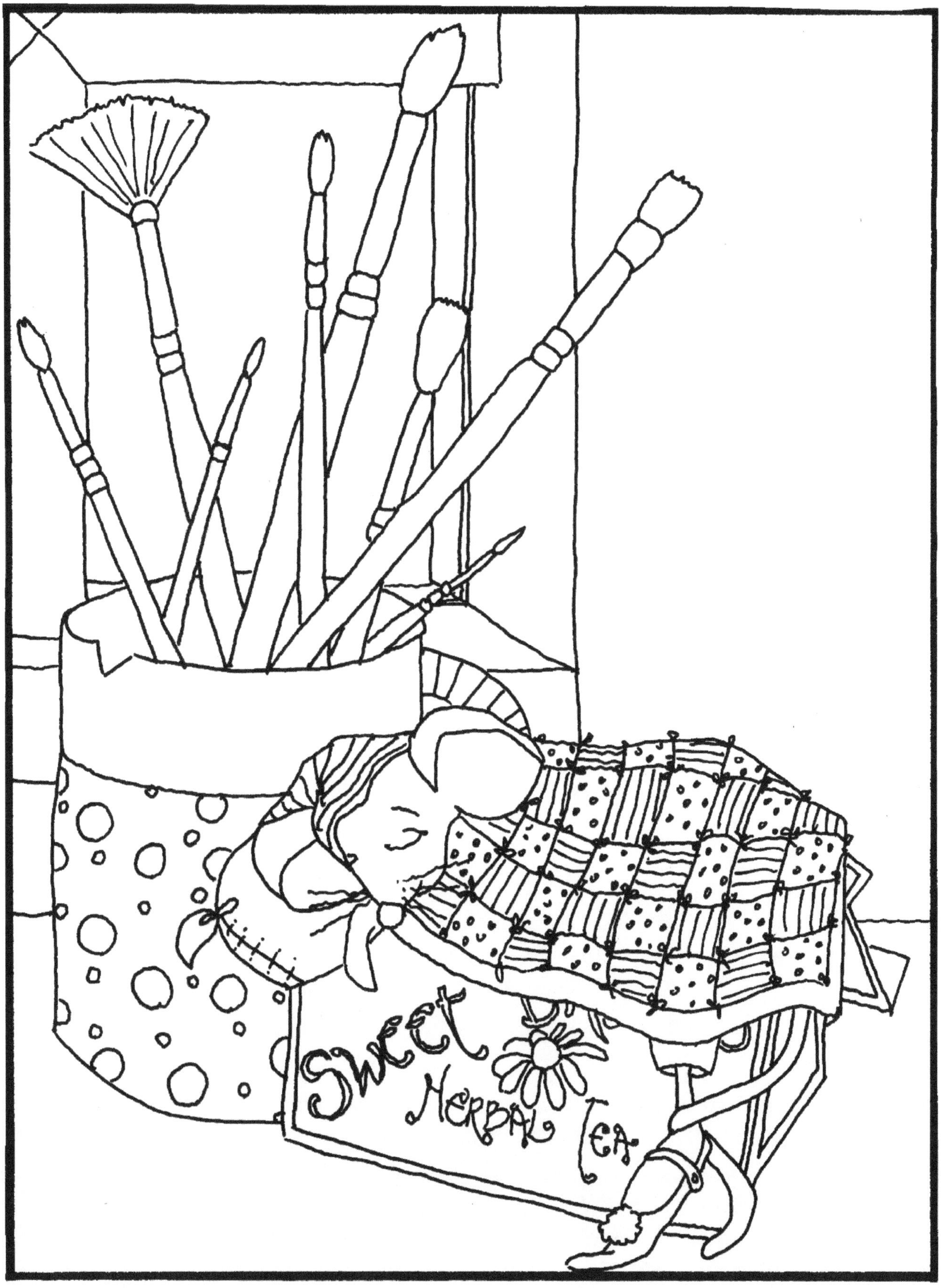
Sweet
HERBAL TEA

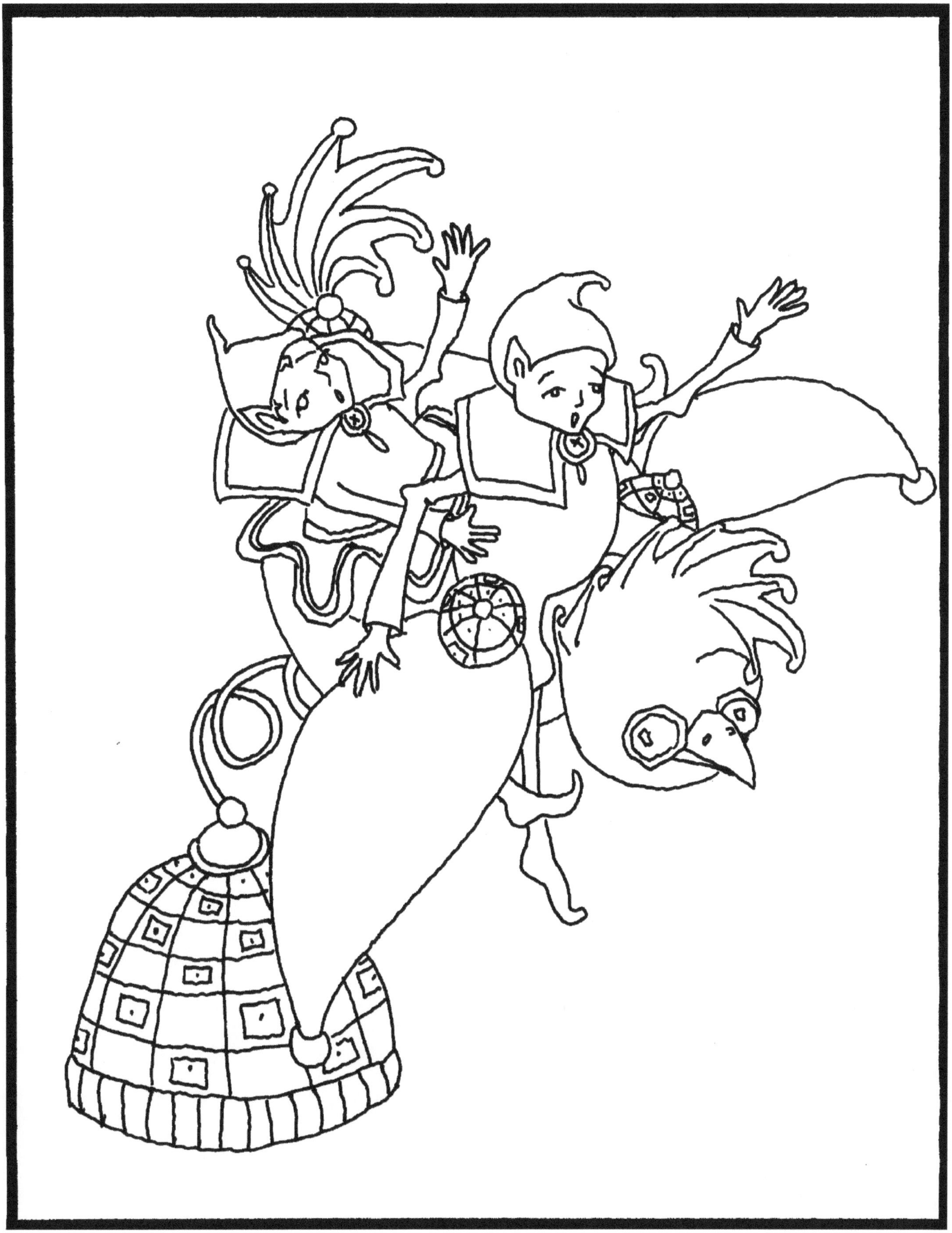

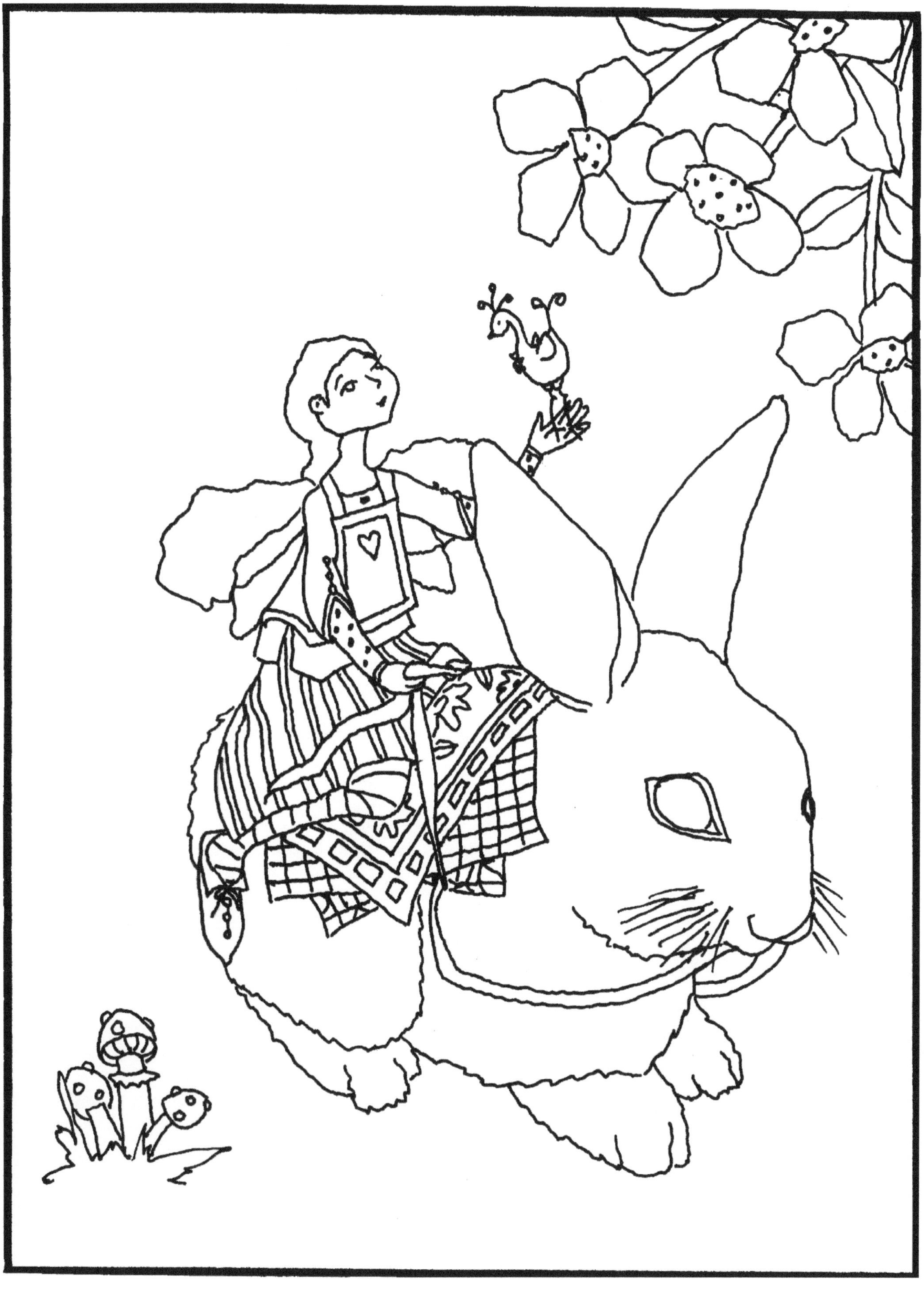

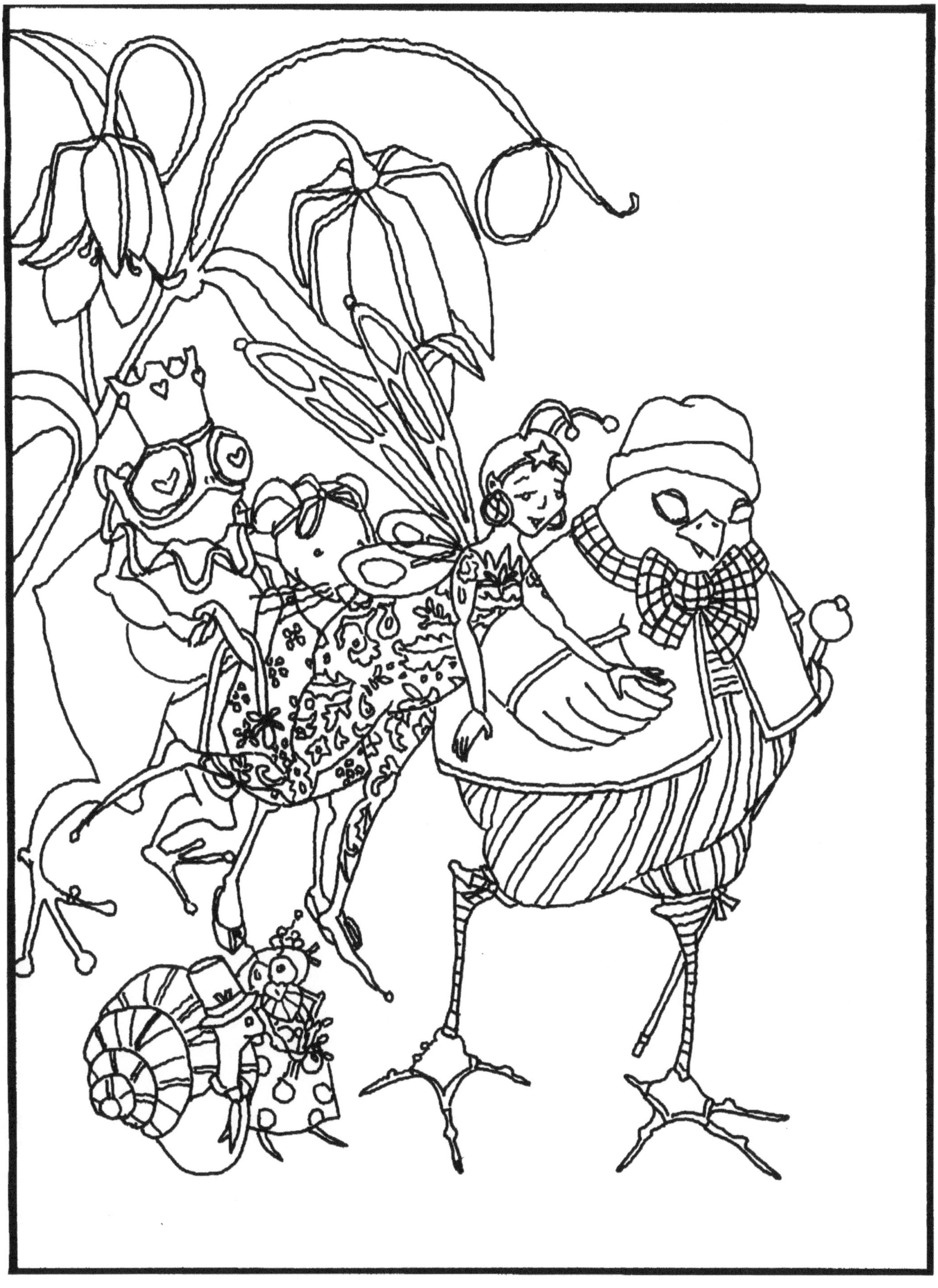

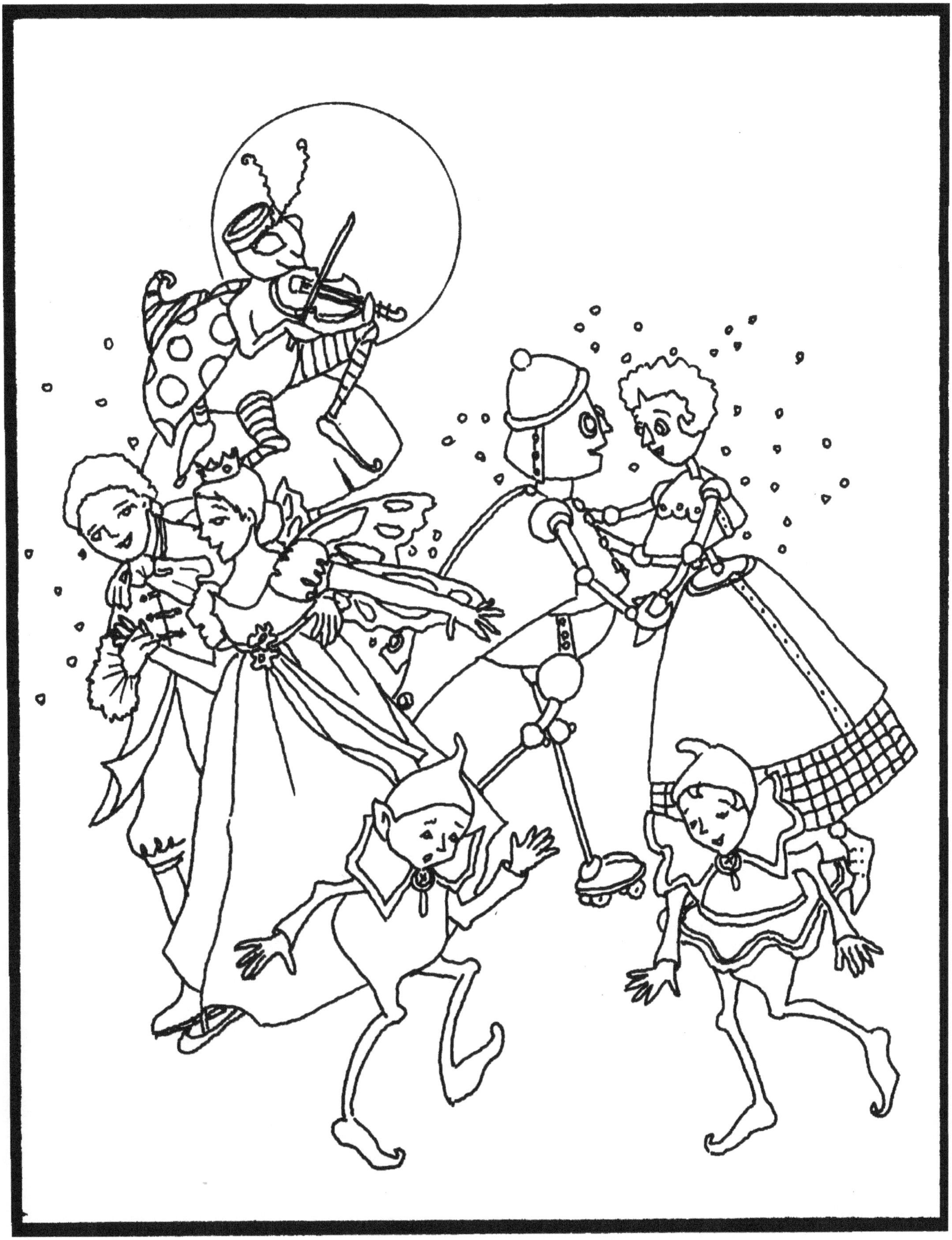

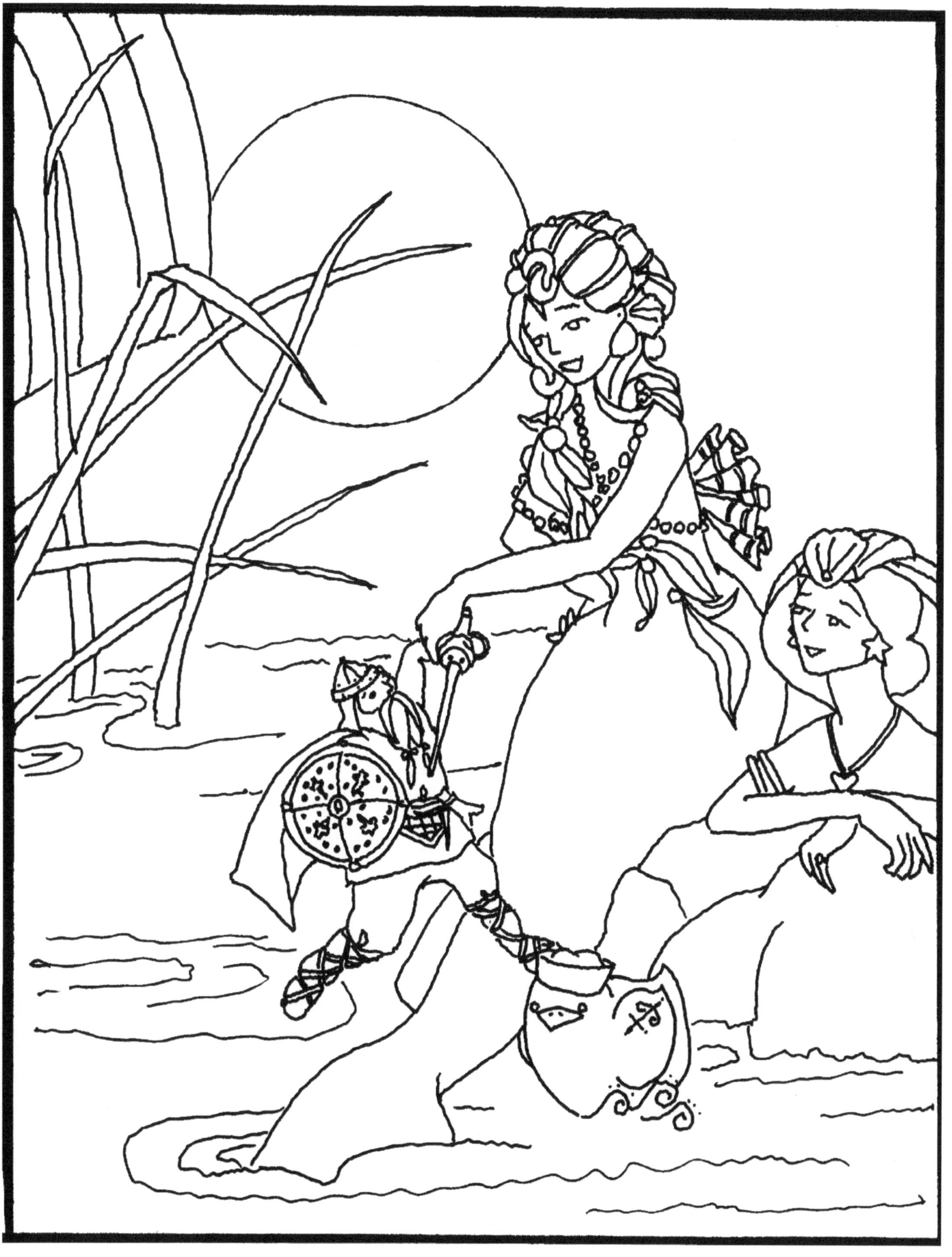

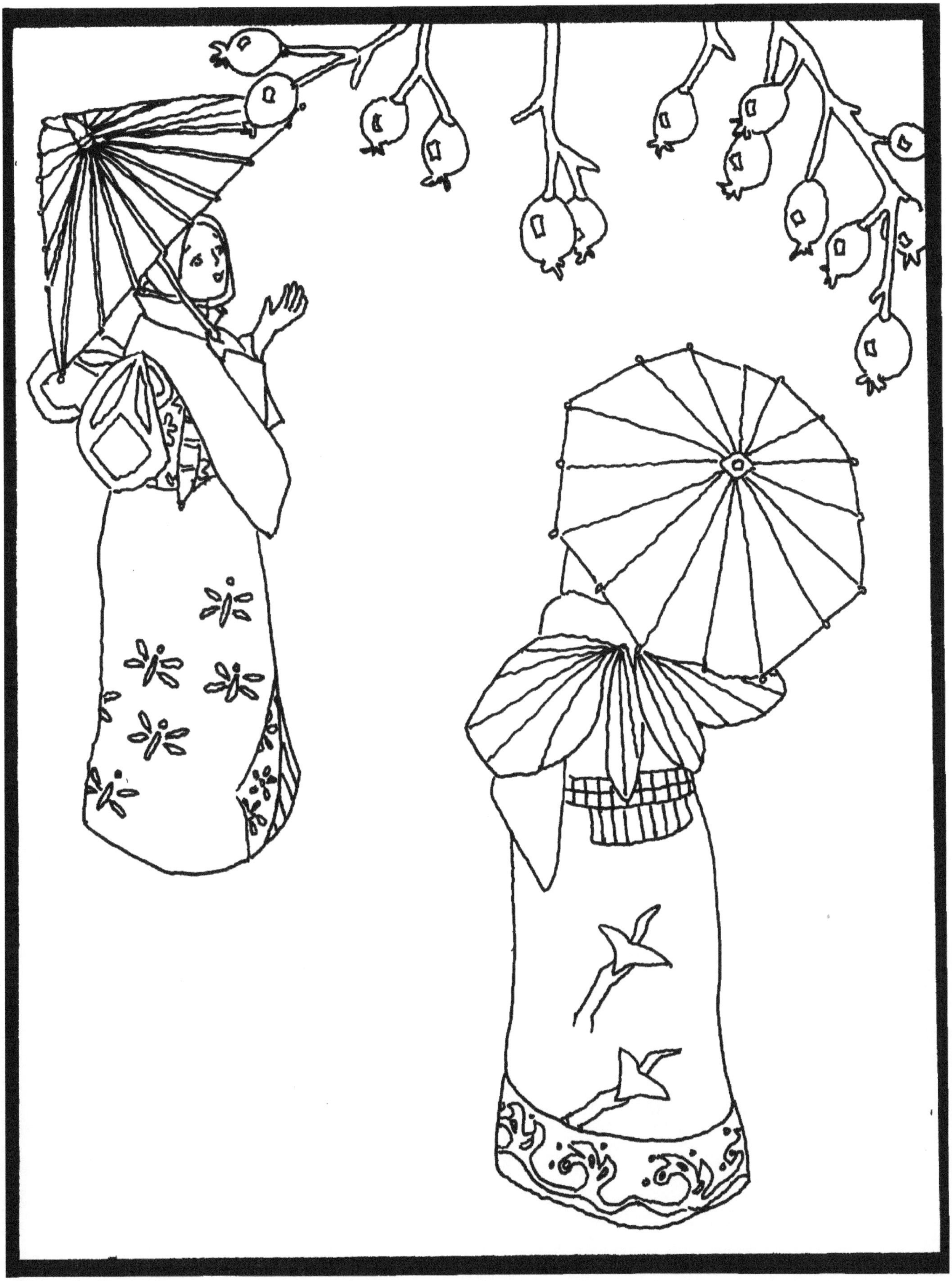

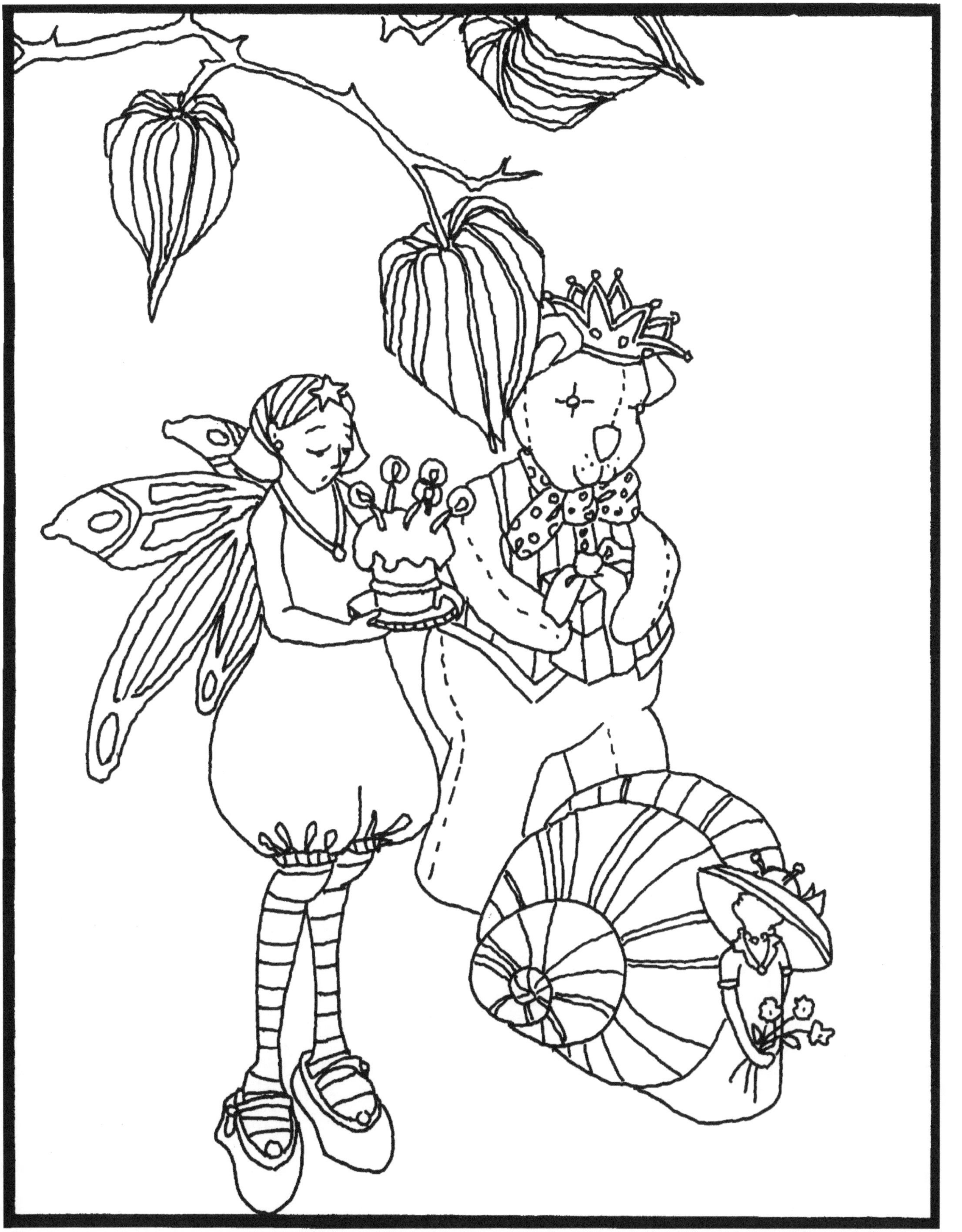

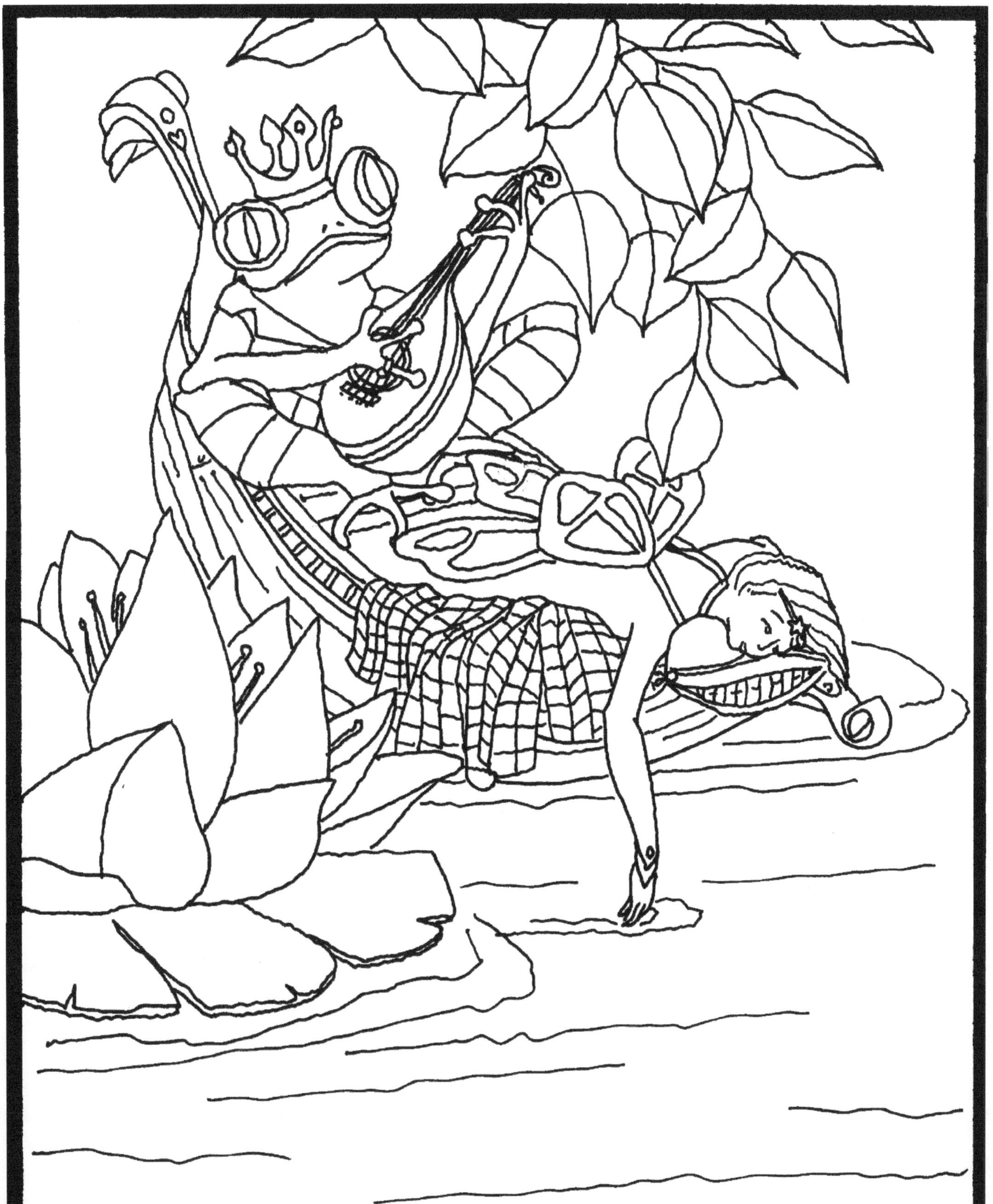

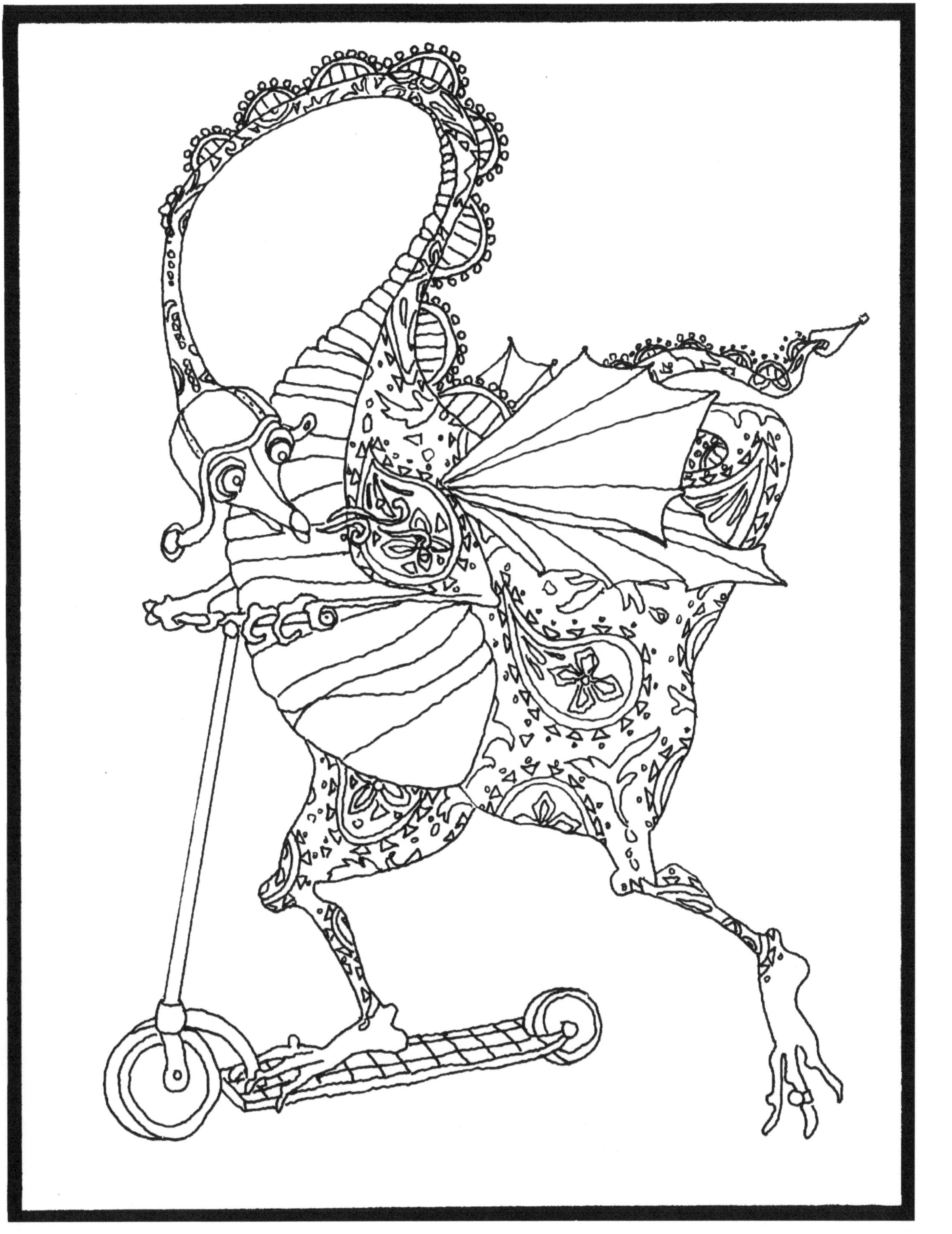

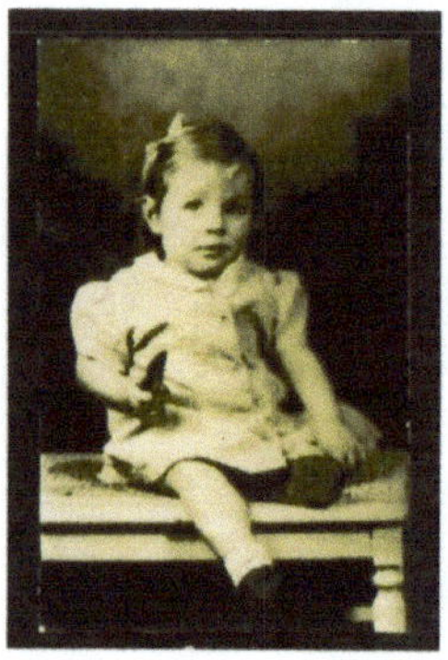

LAURELADEL@GMAIL.COM

laurelnelsonwhimsy.imagekind.com

www.ingramcontent.com/pod-product-compliance
Lightning Source LLC
Chambersburg PA
CBHW050427180526
45159CB00005B/2439
9781537371870